MW01234361

Receiving Healing and Comfort from the Savior

ISBN 978-0-557-05196-0

This book is dedicated to all of the wonderful mommies I have met through the Crabapple First Baptist Church MOPS group over the last four years. Working with you has been such a blessing, and I love watching how God is growing all of us. I love you all very much.

Contents

Introduction

Introduction

In the Gospels, we meet a woman who is so desperate to be healed that she says to herself, "If only I could touch the hem of His cloak, I will be healed." That is what this book is, an attempt to just grasp one edge of His cloak, that we might receive healing, cleansing, and comfort in this journey as a mom. I am not a theologian or an impressive teacher. I am a mother just like you. These are stories that have touched me and enriched my understanding of God's will for my life.

The Bible is the ultimate guidebook for parents, and Jesus has a special place in His heart for mothers. His Word tells us so. These stories of compassion, faith and healing all speak directly to us as mothers. My hope and prayer for you is that these devotionals will enhance your walk and relationship with our Lord and Savior, Jesus Christ.

Many devotional books are written for daily use, offering a passage of Scripture along with insight from the author for application to your life. This book is a little different, though should still be used as a devotional guide. My pastor, Jerry Dockery, has taught me that Scripture is something to be meditated on, mulled over, and analyzed in order to have its greatest impact on us. He calls that "chewing" on it, but I think it's what the psalmist wrote about in 119:15

> I will meditate on Your precepts
> And regard Your ways.

You will be able to use this book for six weeks of meditation and learning. Each week, there is a passage of Scripture that is broken down into five parts, one for each day of your busy week as a mom, Monday through Friday. Not that I suggest you take Saturday and Sunday off, but I understand your obligations and that sometimes your days of rest can be the least restful for you and your family. Each day a specific element of God's Word will be emphasized, and as the Spirit has revealed things to me, I will share them with you. This book is ideal for your busy life, Mom. You can allow God's Word to pour over you daily, and meditate on different aspects of Jesus' teaching and love. I hope this is a blessing to you.

Week One: Jesus Heals a Bleeding Woman (Mark 5:25-34)

Day One:
Suffering Long (Mark 5:25)

25A woman who had had a hemorrhage for twelve years,

26and had endured much at the hands of many physicians, and had spent all that she had and was not helped at all, but rather had grown worse——

27after hearing about Jesus, she came up in the crowd behind Him and touched His cloak.

28For she thought, "If I just touch His garments, I will get well."

29Immediately the flow of her blood was dried up; and she felt in her body that she was healed of her affliction.

30Immediately Jesus, perceiving in Himself that the power proceeding from Him had gone forth, turned around in the crowd and said, "Who touched My garments?"

31And His disciples said to Him, "You see the crowd pressing in on You, and You say, 'Who touched Me?'"

32And He looked around to see the woman who had done this.

33But the woman fearing and trembling, aware of what had happened to her, came and fell down before Him and told Him the whole truth.

34And He said to her, "Daughter, your faith has made you well; go in peace and be healed of your affliction."

- ***Daily Truth***
This woman had been bleeding constantly for twelve years! Her condition must have been related to a reproductive disorder, as any other hemorrhage would have killed her. Can you put yourself in her shoes? Many of us know women and moms who have struggled with reproductive issues for years. This kind of medical problem has existed for millennia, and it matters very much to God. There is no issue too personal or private for Jesus to care about!

  Any issue of blood during this period in history would make a Jewish person ceremonially unclean, and extra-menstrual issues were specified by law as making women unclean, meaning they could not be a part of their congregation. Anyone who dared to go near or touch her would also have been deemed unclean. This woman was most likely socially isolated, as well as spiritually isolated.

25Now if a woman has a discharge of her blood many days, not at the period of her menstrual impurity, or if she has a discharge beyond that period, all the days of her impure discharge she shall continue as though in her menstrual impurity; she is unclean.

26'Any bed on which she lies all the days of her discharge shall be to her like her bed at menstruation; and every thing on which she sits shall be unclean, like her uncleanness at that time.

27'Likewise, whoever touches them shall be unclean and shall wash his clothes and bathe in water and be unclean until evening.

Leviticus 15:25-27

- ***Mothering Moment***
  We can suffer from conditions or afflictions for years that make us feel isolated and alone. Many times, just being a mom can make us feel alone, but God sees us, and cares for us. Whatever problem or struggle we face, we are most likely not alone, and this lesson shows us that God knows and cares about all of the problems we face.

  Today, as you read this passage, is there something you have been dealing with for an extended period of time, health related or otherwise? Take a moment to reflect and write it down, along with the today's date.

Praying Together

Father God, this woman suffered for a long time. She was alone, and cast out, for twelve years. I can't imagine how she must have felt about life, or about You, Lord. I feel alone when I go for a week without seeing any friends, yet there are no rules preventing me from gathering with other people. Thank you for that. Help me to remember the circumstances of other people, and help me to notice when someone is feeling alone. I pray for all the people in my life, Lord, who have suffered illness for an extended time. I know that you will extend Your hands to them, and if it is Your will, please show me how I can be useful to You in bringing comfort. Amen.

Week One: Jesus Heals a Bleeding Woman (Mark 5:25-34)

Day Two:
I've Done All I Can Do (Mark 5:26)

25A woman who had had a hemorrhage for twelve years,

26and had endured much at the hands of many physicians, and had spent all that she had and was not helped at all, but rather had grown worse—

27after hearing about Jesus, she came up in the crowd behind Him and touched His cloak.

28For she thought, "If I just touch His garments, I will get well."

29Immediately the flow of her blood was dried up; and she felt in her body that she was healed of her affliction.

30Immediately Jesus, perceiving in Himself that the power proceeding from Him had gone forth, turned around in the crowd and said, "Who touched My garments?"

31And His disciples said to Him, "You see the crowd pressing in on You, and You say, 'Who touched Me?'"

32And He looked around to see the woman who had done this.

33But the woman fearing and trembling, aware of what had happened to her, came and fell down before Him and told Him the whole truth.

34And He said to her, "Daughter, your faith has made you well; go in peace and be healed of your affliction."

- ***Daily Truth***

  This woman sought medical attention from many physicians. She had spent all of her money on all of the medical attention, and kept getting worse. Spending her time, energy and money on "expert opinions" had only made her worse. This woman was desperate. She was seeking help at her own risk, since she was not allowed by law to be around other Jewish people.

8It is better to take refuge in the LORD
    Than to trust in man.
9It is better to take refuge in the LORD
    Than to trust in princes.
Psalm 118:8-9

28He who trusts in his riches will fall,
But the righteous will flourish like the green leaf.
Proverbs 11:28

- ***Mothering Moment***
  We usually spend all our time and money trying to get ourselves out of problems, medical or

otherwise. We work until we come to the end of our abilities and resources. Is there an area in my life in which I am more willing to trust the "experts" than I am to trust the Lord? Is there an aspect of motherhood that I will spend time and money on until I figure it out?

Praying Together
Lord, please show me what is going on in my life that I am looking for "the experts" to fix. I know that you have put people on this earth and given them skills and insights in order to help others, but I believe that You should be the first one I come to with any questions. When I start looking around for help in any area of my life, please remind me that you are above all things, My Father, and that you are my source for all comfort and strength. Amen.

Week One: Jesus Heals a Bleeding Woman (Mark 5:25-34)

Day Three:
Reaching for the Hem (Mark 5:27-28)

25A woman who had had a hemorrhage for twelve years,

26and had endured much at the hands of many physicians, and had spent all that she had and was not helped at all, but rather had grown worse—

27after hearing about Jesus, she came up in the crowd behind Him and touched His cloak.

28For she thought, "If I just touch His garments, I will get well."

29Immediately the flow of her blood was dried up; and she felt in her body that she was healed of her affliction.

30Immediately Jesus, perceiving in Himself that the power proceeding from Him had gone forth, turned around in the crowd and said, "Who touched My garments?"

31And His disciples said to Him, "You see the crowd pressing in on You, and You say, 'Who touched Me?'"

32And He looked around to see the woman who had done this.

33But the woman fearing and trembling, aware of what had happened to her, came and fell down before Him and told Him the whole truth.

34And He said to her, "Daughter, your faith has made you well; go in peace and be healed of your affliction."

- ***Daily Truth***

    She heard about Him, and went to see if He could heal her, maybe not knowing anything about Him other than hearing He could heal. She chose to believe He was sent from God, and could do the miraculous. The Jewish people were accustomed to doing things, taking action, to seek God's favor, like offering sacrifices for gifts and atonement to God. She knew that taking action to get near Jesus would be beneficial to her.

10for He had healed many, with the result that all those who had afflictions pressed around Him in order to touch Him.
Mark 3:10

23Jesus was going throughout all Galilee, teaching in their synagogues and proclaiming the gospel of the kingdom, and healing every kind of disease and every kind of sickness among the people.
Matthew 4:23

- ***Mothering Moment***

Do I choose, as this woman did, to believe that Jesus can heal me, or my children or family, or whatever is broken, then choose to seek Him out? Am I this trusting? Do I think that getting close to Him will heal me? By taking part in a church community, am I seeking to get nearer to God and feel His power in my life? How can we touch His garment? For those of us in the body of Christ, how can we act like His garment for a hurting and sick world?

Praying Together
Jesus, My Savior, I know about You! I have heard Your voice, and I know what You are able to do. When I spend time with You in prayer and in Your Word, Lord, You make me well. Thank you. I love You.
Amen.

Week One: Jesus Heals a Bleeding Woman (Mark 5:25-34)

Day Four:
His Power Goes Forth (Mark 5:30-32)

25A woman who had had a hemorrhage for twelve years,

26and had endured much at the hands of many physicians, and had spent all that she had and was not helped at all, but rather had grown worse—

27after hearing about Jesus, she came up in the crowd behind Him and touched His cloak.

28For she thought, "If I just touch His garments, I will get well."

29Immediately the flow of her blood was dried up; and she felt in her body that she was healed of her affliction.

30**Immediately Jesus, perceiving in Himself that the power proceeding from Him had gone forth, turned around in the crowd and said, "Who touched My garments?"**

31**And His disciples said to Him, "You see the crowd pressing in on You, and You say, 'Who touched Me?'"**

32And He looked around to see the woman who had done this.

33But the woman fearing and trembling, aware of what had happened to her, came and fell down before Him and told Him the whole truth.

34And He said to her, "Daughter, your faith has made you well; go in peace and be healed of your affliction."

- ***Daily Truth***
  She touched His garment and was healed, and Jesus knew it. He wanted to acknowledge the woman and give her His time and attention. The disciples were confused at why He wanted to know who touched Him, because a large crowd was around Him, pressing in and touching Him. There was probably not a whole lot of room to make forward progress. But He was making a statement about how each and every one of us are important to Him. He doesn't just see a crowd, He sees the faces in the crowd.

17One day He was teaching; and there were some Pharisees and teachers of the law sitting there, who had come from every village of Galilee and Judea and from Jerusalem; and the power of the Lord was present for Him to perform healing.
Luke 5:17

19And all the people were trying to touch Him, for power was coming from Him and healing them all.
Luke 6:19

- ***Mothering Moment***
  He heals. There is power proceeding from Him, and He wants to give attention to each one of us who asks. When we go to the Lord in prayer, He hears us and knows us when we come with a believing and trusting heart. He wants to pay attention to us. He has all power and authority, and longs for us to reach out and trust him. Is your prayer life one of trust and belief?

Praying Together
Thank you, Lord Jesus, for wanting to know about me. You know all things, yet You love for me to confide everything in You. Thank you for speaking to me, for loving me, choosing me, and dying for me.
Amen.

Week One: Jesus Heals a Bleeding Woman (Mark 5:25-34)
Day Five:
Your Faith Has Made You Well

25A woman who had had a hemorrhage for twelve years,

26and had endured much at the hands of many physicians, and had spent all that she had and was not helped at all, but rather had grown worse—

27after hearing about Jesus, she came up in the crowd behind Him and touched His cloak.

28For she thought, "If I just touch His garments, I will get well."

29Immediately the flow of her blood was dried up; and she felt in her body that she was healed of her affliction.

30Immediately Jesus, perceiving in Himself that the power proceeding from Him had gone forth, turned around in the crowd and said, "Who touched My garments?"

31And His disciples said to Him, "You see the crowd pressing in on You, and You say, 'Who touched Me?'"

32And He looked around to see the woman who had done this.

33But the woman fearing and trembling, aware of what had happened to her, came and fell down before Him and told Him the whole truth.

34And He said to her, "Daughter, your faith has made you well; go in peace and be healed of your affliction."

- *Daily Truth*
  She knew she had broken the law and touched the healer, and was healed. She knew He was the Messiah. She fell at His feet to worship Him, and confessed to Him. This was a personal moment between the woman and God. Jesus mentions her faith because of the risk she was willing to take, and because she was choosing to believe Him. She had faith enough to get out of her normal routine and rut, to abandon her old habit of doing things, and to trust God. Faith is the act of choosing to believe God, not because of what we have seen, but in spite of not seeing.

1Now faith is the assurance of things hoped for, the conviction of things not seen..
Hebrews 11:1

7for we walk by faith, not by sight—
2 Corinthians 5:7

- *Mothering Moment*
  He is capable of healing all our afflictions, but we cannot receive His power without believing in

Him, and fully trusting in Him. We should approach the Savior in humility and repentance, knowing what He has done and is still doing in our lives. This passage provides a wonderful example of approaching God in prayer. Approaching God in fear and trembling means we take seriously who He is and what He is capable of. Telling Him the whole truth about who and what we are, and where we have been, submits our lives completely to Him, and it is an important step to relinquish any secrets or anything we hold back from Him. If Jesus were to speak to you today, what comment would He make about your faith? Do you trust Him because of what you can see He has done, or because you have not seen but still believe?

Praying Together
Father God, You are the Creator and Redeemer of all. I come to You today, knowing and admitting the iniquity in my heart. I know I am not deserving of Your love and grace, yet You pour it out on me anyway. My faith falters most days, Lord, but I choose to believe that You have the best plans and intentions for me today. Please guide my footsteps, and keep me close to You.
Amen.

Week Two: Jesus Cleanses a Leper (Matthew 8:1-4)

Day One:
Large Crowds Followed (Matthew 8:1)

1When Jesus came down from the mountain, large crowds followed Him.

2And a leper came to Him and bowed down before Him, and said, "Lord, if You are willing, You can make me clean."

3Jesus stretched out His hand and touched him, saying, "I am willing; be cleansed." And immediately his leprosy was cleansed.

4And Jesus said to him, "See that you tell no one; but go, show yourself to the priest and present the offering that Moses commanded, as a testimony to them."

- ***Daily Truth***
  Jesus had just finished giving the Sermon on the Mount, one of His most famous and longest sermons. It probably took several days to cover all of the lessons He taught. He introduced the large crowds to many new concepts, such as the Beatitudes, how to build godly relationships, as well as the advent of salvation in the world. He spent many long hours teaching the Truth, and imparting great wisdom, yet the crowds still wanted more. These people who had just heard

17

the longest sermon ever couldn't get enough!
They followed Him!

These large crowds following Jesus consisted of
His followers and disciples, as well as strangers,
Jews and Gentiles. Today we would term many
of these people "seekers," looking for God and
actively seeking out those who teach about Him.
Alongside those seekers would also have been
many critics, those in the Jewish religious
hierarchy who were waiting for Jesus to make a
mistake.

Due to the length of the passages, I did not print them
here. Go through Matthew, Chapters 5-7 for the
complete Sermon on the Mount.

- *Mothering Moment*
  How many days do you spend pouring out all
  your strength and resources for your children and
  your family? How many wonderful days do you
  get to take advantage of those "teachable
  moments" you have as a mother? During those
  moments, when you think you've just about
  gotten through to your listeners, do they come at
  you with another need or another question?
  Think about potty training, or when your child
  has gone through the "but, why?" stage, or during
  what one of my friends lovingly refers to as
  "homework hell." Jesus has experienced all that
  you have Mom, and more. Imagine what He
  might have been thinking when He concluded the

best sermon ever, just to be followed, hounded by the crowd....

The Lord of the universe was constantly followed, rarely having time alone, even after teaching for a long time and spending days with people. Everyone placed demands on His time. If this is true for Him, shouldn't it be expected for me? What happens when I am pursued and followed?

Praying Together

Lord, You were doggedly pursued all the days of Your ministry. We read in the Gospels about You retreating to pray alone.... You knew very well the demands other people can put on one's life and time. You see us, as mommies, seldom finding a moment of peace, and I know You empathize with us. Thank you, Lord Jesus, for so intimately knowing and understanding my needs. When I am being pursued, and feel as though I can't get a moment of peace, fill me with Your Spirit so I can remember that "even the Son of Man did not come to be served, but to serve, and to give His life a ransom for many."
Amen.

Week Two: Jesus Cleanses a Leper (Matthew 8:1-4)

Day Two:
If You Are Willing (Matthew 8:2)

1When Jesus came down from the mountain, large crowds followed Him.

2And a leper came to Him and bowed down before Him, and said, "Lord, if You are willing, You can make me clean."

3Jesus stretched out His hand and touched him, saying, "I am willing; be cleansed." And immediately his leprosy was cleansed.

4And Jesus said to him, "See that you tell no one; but go, show yourself to the priest and present the offering that Moses commanded, as a testimony to them."

- *Daily Truth*
  Leprosy was a highly contagious bacterial disease causing sores and eventually the deterioration of tissue. Since treatment was most likely not as effective as it is today, many times it led to permanent damage of the nerves, skin, eyes and limbs. Lepers were considered to be ritually unclean according to Mosaic law. Like the woman from last week, this man was really going out on a limb socially. Leprosy was contagious, and contact was prohibited between infected and

non-infected people. This man was shunned,
shut-out, and in a great deal of discomfort.

Can you imagine what the crowds must have
been thinking? "Oh, no, it's a leper! Don't let
him touch me! What if he infects Jesus? Keep
him away!" Though the Lord would show great
mercy toward this man, do you think the crowd
was loving and understanding? After all, it was
against the law for him to be around people.

*8"The priest shall look, and if the scab has spread on the
skin, then the priest shall pronounce him unclean; it is
leprosy.*
Leviticus 13:8

*45"As for the leper who has the infection, his clothes
shall be torn, and the hair of his head shall be
uncovered, and he shall cover his mustache and cry,
'Unclean! Unclean!'*

*46"He shall remain unclean all the days during which he
has the infection; he is unclean.*
*He shall live alone; his dwelling shall be outside the
camp."*
Leviticus 13:45-46

- **Mothering Moment**
  The leper was an outcast, yet bowed down to
  honor Jesus, placing Christ above all else,

including his circumstances. He also placed God's will above his own need, asking if Jesus was willing to make him clean.

There may not be a physical ailment that makes you "unclean", but what about an attitude of your heart or your mind? Unforgiveness, or a broken relationship, can cause deterioration just like a disease can. Have I asked Jesus if He is willing to make me clean?

Praying Together
Father God, You see all of the things inside me, and in my life, that make me unclean. Please, Lord, point them out to me so that I cannot ignore them. Show me Your will, Lord, and if there are attitudes and actions making me unclean, please take them away. Only let Your will be done, Lord God, not mine.
Amen.

Week Two: Jesus Cleanses a Leper (Matthew 8:1-4)
Day Three:
I Am Willing (Matthew 8:3)

1When Jesus came down from the mountain, large crowds followed Him.

2And a leper came to Him and bowed down before Him, and said, "Lord, if You are willing, You can make me clean."

3Jesus stretched out His hand and touched him, saying, "I am willing; be cleansed." And immediately his leprosy was cleansed.

4And Jesus said to him, "See that you tell no one; but go, show yourself to the priest and present the offering that Moses commanded, as a testimony to them."

- *Daily Truth*
  The first thing Jesus did was take action, and radical action. He touched a leper; unthinkable to most people. And He healed him! He *was* willing. He helped the man because He could, and because He wanted to.

  According to Leviticus chapter 13, the priests had no special ability to heal, rather they could determine whether the infection was unclean or not. Jesus did not just tell the man what his problem was, or confirm his diagnosis, He healed him. Jesus is not like any other, and this man saw that . The leper came seeking to be cleansed, not seeking advice or instruction.

- *Mothering Moment*
Jesus takes radical action when His help is sought. Do we do the same with our own family and friends? What about with strangers?

The most logical and practical thing a priest could do was tell a person what they already knew, and then how to cope with it. That is what the world offers us and our families, diagnosis and coping skills. How do you approach a need? As an "armchair quarterback," spouting out the obvious and giving suggestions, or would you step out and take action? Do I open myself up to God and the church to take radical action in my life?

Praying Together
Lord God, You said "I am willing; be cleansed." You said that You are willing, not only that, but able, to cleanse our most horrible ills. Thank You, Lord! You stretch out your hands to me, to everyone, to anyone willing to call You, and You say "I am willing." There is nothing You are not willing to heal or cleanse. Help me, my Father, to tell everyone I see that You are willing. You have healed me. I praise Your name.
Amen.

Week Two: Jesus Cleanses a Leper (Matthew 8:1-4)

Day Four:
Telling (Matthew 8:4)

1When Jesus came down from the mountain, large crowds followed Him.

2And a leper came to Him and bowed down before Him, and said, "Lord, if You are willing, You can make me clean."

3Jesus stretched out His hand and touched him, saying, "I am willing; be cleansed." And immediately his leprosy was cleansed.

4**And Jesus said to him, "See that you tell no one**; but go, show yourself to the priest and present the offering that Moses commanded, as a testimony to them."

- *Daily Truth*
  Why would Jesus not want to let anyone know what He had done? He might have been taken to task for breaking the law by some of the Jewish leadership, giving them a reason to stop His ministry. The people may have started to riot in the streets if the large crowds had heard and seen and understood. It simply was not the right time for His Divinity to be revealed.

  How might the leper have understood Jesus? If I had been in his shoes, I would have wanted to tell everyone and show everyone that I had been miraculously cleansed by my Lord! This man knew, however, that he had not followed the procedures given in law and enacted by the priests. It may not have been the requisite seven days of purification, so the priests would have been skeptical as to his cleanliness. Maybe the leper didn't understand what Jesus wanted at all, but still chose to obey Him.

9Departing from there, He went into their synagogue.

10And a man was there whose hand was withered. And they questioned Jesus, asking, "Is it lawful to heal on the Sabbath?"--so that they might accuse Him.

11And He said to them, "What man is there among you who has a sheep, and if it falls into a pit on the Sabbath, will he not take hold of it and lift it out?

12"How much more valuable then is a man than a sheep! So then, it is lawful to do good on the Sabbath."

13Then He said to the man, "Stretch out your hand!" He stretched it out, and it was restored to normal, like the other.

14But the Pharisees went out and conspired against Him, as to how they might destroy Him.

15But Jesus, aware of this, withdrew from there. Many followed Him, and He healed them all,

16and warned them not to tell who He was.

Matthew 12:9-16

13Now when Jesus came into the district of Caesarea Philippi, He was asking His disciples, "Who do people say that the Son of Man is?"

14And they said, "Some say John the Baptist; and others, Elijah; but still others, Jeremiah, or one of the prophets."

15He said to them, "But who do you say that I am?"

16Simon Peter answered, "You are the Christ, the Son of the living God."

17And Jesus said to him, "Blessed are you, Simon Barjona, because flesh and blood did not reveal this to you, but My Father who is in heaven.

18"I also say to you that you are Peter, and upon this rock I will build My church; and the gates of Hades will not overpower it.

19"I will give you the keys of the kingdom of heaven; and whatever you bind on earth shall have been bound in

27

heaven, and whatever you loose on earth shall have been loosed in heaven."

20Then He warned the disciples that they should tell no one that He was the Christ.

Matthew 16:13-20

- **Mothering Moment**
  We don't have to keep His miraculous power secret. His earthly ministry is finished for now, and His work on the cross promises His return. Now we need to make Him known to everyone. Can you think of any occasion in which you have kept Jesus' work for you under wraps? Can you think of any situation that would make sense to do that?

Praying Together
Lord, please give me a spirit of boldness in sharing the news of Your good works in my life with everyone. I am not ashamed of You, and thank You for allowing me to live in a free society where I can tell anyone and everyone all about You. Help me to understand the mysteries contained in Your Word, and to give me peace when there are things I can't understand. Empower me by Your Holy Spirit to obey even what I don't understand.
Amen.

Week Two: Jesus Cleanses a Leper (Matthew 8:1-4)

Day Five:
As a Testimony to Them (Matthew8:4)

1When Jesus came down from the mountain, large crowds followed Him.

2And a leper came to Him and bowed down before Him, and said, "Lord, if You are willing, You can make me clean."

3Jesus stretched out His hand and touched him, saying, "I am willing: be cleansed." And immediately his leprosy was cleansed.

4And Jesus said to him, "See that you tell no one: **but go, show yourself to the priest and present the offering that Moses commanded, as a testimony to them."**

- *Daily Truth*
  Jesus commanded the man to follow the procedure set forth in law to prove that he had indeed been cleansed. He also told him to give an offering to God, also prescribed in the law. Jesus wanted the priests and others to know this man was clean, and He wanted God to be honored and glorified.

  Jesus was encouraging a fellow Jew to follow the law, not to break it. By following the law, the man who had formerly had leprosy, would be testifying of God's greatness to the priests and to the whole congregation. He would be allowed back into the congregation to worship, and could tell people what God had done.

17"Do not think that I came to abolish the Law or the Prophets; I did not come to abolish but to fulfill."
Matthew 5:17

- ***Mothering Moment***
Though not all were ready to accept Jesus as the Christ, they all still needed to see the result of His work. We all have people in our lives who are not ready to accept Him, but need to see Jesus at work in our lives, in our mothering and in the way we treat our families and others.

  Jesus told the man that the fact he was cleansed would be "a testimony to them." Think of what Jesus has done or is doing in your life that can be a testimony to all people around you. Can your children, your friends and your family see that God is at work in your life? What is your testimony to them about Jesus?

Praying Together
Father God, there are days that pass by without even a thought of what my testimony is to those around me. Even my closest family and friends can't see what You are doing in my life, because I'm not telling them. I

don't live my life as a testimony to them. I am so sorry. Thank you for forgiving me. Thank you for giving me another day to testify about Your greatness. Lord Jesus, I want to tell everyone I know about your power in my life. Please show me opportunities all around me. Thank you for giving me a testimony. Thank you for renewing my life.
Amen.

Week Three: Jesus Heals a Paralytic (Matthew 9:1-8)
Day One:
They Brought Their Friend (Matthew 9:1-2)

1Getting into a boat, Jesus crossed over the sea and came to His own city.

2And they brought to Him a paralytic lying on a bed. Seeing their faith, Jesus said to the paralytic, "Take courage, son; your sins are forgiven."

3And some of the scribes said to themselves, "This fellow blasphemes."

4And Jesus knowing their thoughts said, "Why are you thinking evil in your hearts?

5Which is easier, to say, 'Your sins are forgiven,' or to say, 'Get up, and walk'?

6But so that you may know that the Son of Man has authority on earth to forgive sins"--then He said to the paralytic, "Get up, pick up your bed and go home."

7And he got up and went home.

8But when the crowds saw this, they were awestruck, and glorified God, who had given such authority to men.

- ***Daily Truth***
  Jesus was in His hometown, Nazareth. In other Gospel accounts, it was in Nazareth where He

was rejected by the people who knew Him. In this instance, people were seeking Him out - a carpenter's son, Mary's first born – so they could bring their ailing loved ones to Him.

The paralytic's friends had previously encountered Jesus. Though there is no exact account of who they were and what they believed, it is clear by this story that they knew who Jesus was. They convinced their friend, the paralyzed man, to allow them to carry him on his bed through the streets and into the crowd which surrounded Jesus. They knew Jesus could help him, and they did their best to show him.

2Now the feast of the Jews, the Feast of Booths, was near.
3Therefore His brothers said to Him, "Leave here and go into Judea, so that Your disciples also may see Your works which You are doing.
4"For no one does anything in secret when he himself seeks to be known publicly. If You do these things, show Yourself to the world."
5For not even His brothers were believing in Him.

John 7:2-5

20And He came home, and the crowd gathered again, to such an extent that they could not even eat a meal.
21When His own people heard of this, they went out to

take custody of Him; for they were saying, "He has lost His senses."

Mark 3:20-21

- **Mothering Moment**
  Do I have friends I want to convince that Jesus will help them? Will I carry them to Him?

  Am I willing to carry my children or my husband to Jesus? Have I done what I can to convince those closest to me that He is the Savior? How can I practically implement a lifestyle of carrying my loved ones to Jesus?

Praying Together
Father God, I confess that I have not carried all of my loved ones to You. It is more of a matter of convenience sometimes than anything else. But the testimony You are showing us in the friends of this man.... They were not deterred by crowds, circumstances, or any sense of inconvenience. They knew You could heal their friend, and they wanted to see that happen. Lord, I know you can heal my friends, and I want to see that happen. Help me to find ways to carry them to You, no matter the cost to me.
Amen.

Week Three: Jesus Heals a Paralytic (Matthew 9:1-8)
Day Two:
Seeing Their Faith (Matthew 9:2)

1Getting into a boat, Jesus crossed over the sea and came to His own city.

2And they brought to Him a paralytic lying on a bed. **Seeing their faith, Jesus said to the paralytic, "Take courage, son; your sins are forgiven."**

3And some of the scribes said to themselves, "This fellow blasphemes."

4And Jesus knowing their thoughts said, "Why are you thinking evil in your hearts?

5"Which is easier, to say, 'Your sins are forgiven,' or to say, 'Get up, and walk'?

6"But so that you may know that the Son of Man has authority on earth to forgive sins"--then He said to the paralytic, "Get up, pick up your bed and go home."

7And he got up and went home.

8But when the crowds saw this, they were awestruck, and glorified God, who had given such authority to men.

- *Daily Truth*
  In answer to the faith of a man's friends, Jesus was willing to forgive his sins. The faith of a few

good friends gave hope to a hopeless man. *Their faith* caused their friend to come to Jesus. *Their faith* caused an opportunity for Jesus to minister. Jesus is always willing to forgive anyone of any sin. His work on the cross accomplished the forgiveness of all sins! This was a moment for Him to demonstrate His authority to forgive.

The paralytic was brought to Jesus to be healed, but Jesus instead said first that his sins were forgiven. This was probably a surprise to the men, not to mention the surrounding crowd.

5for our gospel did not come to you in word only, but also in power and in the Holy Spirit and with full conviction; just as you know what kind of men we proved to be among you for your sake.

6You also became imitators of us and of the Lord, having received the word in much tribulation with the joy of the Holy Spirit,

I Thessalonians 1:5-6

- ***Mothering Moment***
  We can surmise from this story, because the paralyzed man was actually present, that he had become convinced of Jesus' healing ability. He did not get what he expected, though. Did he know his sins needed to be forgiven?

How many times do we ask Jesus' help, without first addressing our sin? Why did Jesus make a point of addressing sin first?

Praying Together
Lord God, my unconfessed sin sometimes hangs like a wall between us. When I fail to recognize that I have not done the things I should, and done things I should not have; when I fail to recognize Your power and presence and sovereignty in and over my life, I can't get close to You. Prick my heart, Father God, when I am out of Your will and in sin. Make my soul burn inside me when I am not in submission to Your authority, so I can repent, and turn away from the thing that gets between us. I do not want anything to stand between us. Show me, and I will confess it, and I will repent, and You will create in me a clean heart, O God, and renew a steadfast spirit within me.
Amen.

Week Three: Jesus Heals a Paralytic (Matthew 9:1-8)

Day Three:
Which Is Easier? (Matthew 9:3-5)

1Getting into a boat, Jesus crossed over the sea and came to His own city.

2And they brought to Him a paralytic lying on a bed. Seeing their faith, Jesus said to the paralytic, "Take courage, son; your sins are forgiven."

3And some of the scribes said to themselves, "This fellow blasphemes."

4And Jesus knowing their thoughts said, "Why are you thinking evil in your hearts?

5"Which is easier, to say, 'Your sins are forgiven,' or to say, 'Get up, and walk'?

6"But so that you may know that the Son of Man has authority on earth to forgive sins"--then He said to the paralytic, "Get up, pick up your bed and go home."

7And he got up and went home.

8But when the crowds saw this, they were awestruck, and glorified God, who had given such authority to men.

- ***Daily Truth***

  Which is an easier thing for Jesus to accomplish? He forgives our sins, past, present, and future, and is able to make us whole and heal us. He asked this question to really point out that all He did was amazing and seemingly impossible. It only could be accomplished by God.

  The forgiveness of sins was only ritually accomplished by the priests when they administered the offerings brought by people who acknowledged their sins. God would forgive sins when a sacrifice was offered. But the people had no intimate connection with God that would allow reconciliation between the sin they had committed and a peaceful soul. When John the Baptist came prophesying about Jesus, he preached about repentance and the forgiveness of sins. Jesus himself told people to confess and turn away from their sins because He had brought about the kingdom of heaven.

1Now in those days John the Baptist came, preaching in the wilderness of Judea, saying,

2"Repent, for the kingdom of heaven is at hand."

Matthew 3:1-2

14Now after John had been taken into custody, Jesus came into Galilee, preaching the gospel of God,

15and saying, "The time is fulfilled, and the kingdom of God is at hand; repent and believe in the gospel."

Mark 1:14-15

- ### *Mothering Moment*
  When we become saved, we ask forgiveness for our sins and receive it. We all look for forgiveness from God, but how often do we look for a changed life in an ongoing way? Being born again is wonderful, and is the first step in a new life. But each time we come to God for forgiveness, He has an opportunity to change us, if we will let Him. Each time I mess up as a mom, and ask God to forgive me, I have a new opportunity to be changed.

  The crowd thought it was easier for Jesus to heal a man than to forgive their sins. He was showing them that forgiveness comes first.

Praying Together
Father God, You have forgiven every sin. You have blotted them out from Your presence. It is a miracle. Each time I come to You with a repentant heart, You can regenerate me again. You can, and want to, change me day by day. Am I living in that knowledge? Help me to remember just what You are doing in my life, and just what You are allowing the Holy Spirit to do through me,

40

each and every time I remember I need Your forgiveness.
I do not just want to go through the motions, Lord. I do
not want to pay you lip service. Change me every day,
my Savior. Make me more like You.
Amen.

Week Three: Jesus Heals a Paralytic (Matthew 9:1-8)

Day Four:
Get Up and Go Home (Matthew 9:6-7)

1Getting into a boat, Jesus crossed over the sea and came to His own city.

2And they brought to Him a paralytic lying on a bed. Seeing their faith, Jesus said to the paralytic, "Take courage, son; your sins are forgiven."

3And some of the scribes said to themselves, "This fellow blasphemes."

4And Jesus knowing their thoughts said, "Why are you thinking evil in your hearts?

5"Which is easier, to say, 'Your sins are forgiven,' or to say, 'Get up, and walk'?

6"But so that you may know that the Son of Man has authority on earth to forgive sins"--then He said to the paralytic, "Get up, pick up your bed and go home."

7And he got up and went home.

8But when the crowds saw this, they were awestruck, and glorified God, who had given such authority to men.

- ***Daily Truth***

  Jesus was showing the crowd who He is. He can do all things.

  The presence of an illness was closely related to sin in most people's minds within the population Jesus was teaching. It was commonly thought that illness was God's punishment for sin. For Jesus to relate the forgiveness of sins to reversing this man's paralysis was communicating directly to the people and their perceptions. Being healed of an affliction would serve as evidence to the people that the man's sins had really been forgiven. Jesus was testifying about Himself.

1As He passed by, He saw a man blind from birth.

2And His disciples asked Him, "Rabbi, who sinned, this man or his parents, that he would be born blind?"

3Jesus answered, "It was neither that this man sinned, nor his parents; but it was so that the works of God might be displayed in him.

4"We must work the works of Him who sent Me as long as it is day; night is coming when no one can work.

5"While I am in the world, I am the Light of the world."

6When He had said this, He spat on the ground, and made clay of the spittle, and applied the clay to his eyes,

*7and said to him, "Go, wash in the pool of Siloam"
(which is translated, Sent.) So he went away and washed,
and came back seeing.*

John 9:1-7

- **Mothering Moment**
  We don't usually associate illness with sin
  anymore. We know that God doesn't punish us,
  though He does judge our sin. Consequences of
  sin may manifest in illness, poverty, or other
  maladies, but the punishment for our sins has
  already been taken care of in Jesus' crucifixion.

  When I come to Jesus to forgive my sins, I know
  they will be forgotten, but by Him, not
  necessarily by me. Many times, I accept His
  forgiveness, but I just continue to lay around on
  my pallet, paralyzed in front of Him. For me, it
  is far easier to comprehend the forgiveness of my
  sins than to understand that I can get up, pick up
  my bed, and go home. I don't intentionally
  wallow around in my sin, but do I really expect to
  be changed, healed, and overcome the obstacles
  before me?

Praying Together
*Lord, so many times, I live day by day, sometimes just
surviving from one crucial situation to the next. My faith
carries me through the difficult moments of motherhood,
but the paralysis that keeps me on my pallet can hang
around for awhile. I know I can expect You to handle*

the situations in my life that I just survive. The temper tantrums (theirs and mine,) the fatigue, worry, illness, chronic conditions…. But more than that, You want me to thrive. You say to me "Daughter, get up, pick that up and go home." Except You say "Come home to Me." You can make me thrive because of Your faithfulness, and because You abide with me. Help me to remember that by Your forgiveness, You empower me to pick up my pallet and walk. Thank you, Lord God.
Amen.

Week Three: Jesus Heals a Paralytic (Matthew 9:1-8)

Day Five:
Awestruck! (Matthew 9:8)

1Getting into a boat, Jesus crossed over the sea and came to His own city.

2And they brought to Him a paralytic lying on a bed. Seeing their faith, Jesus said to the paralytic, "Take courage, son; your sins are forgiven."

3And some of the scribes said to themselves, "This fellow blasphemes."

4And Jesus knowing their thoughts said, "Why are you thinking evil in your hearts?

5"Which is easier, to say, 'Your sins are forgiven,' or to say, 'Get up, and walk'?

6"But so that you may know that the Son of Man has authority on earth to forgive sins"--then He said to the paralytic, "Get up, pick up your bed and go home."

7And he got up and went home.

8But when the crowds saw this, they were awestruck, and glorified God, who had given such authority to men.

- ***Daily Truth***

  The people who witnessed this event were awestruck. They were seeing the impossible.

  The crowds were glorifying God, recognizing that He had sent Jesus to have authority over all things, and that He could forgive all sins.

17When they saw Him, they worshiped Him; but some were doubtful.

18And Jesus came up and spoke to them, saying, "All authority has been given to Me in heaven and on earth.

19"Go therefore and make disciples of all the nations, baptizing them in the name of the Father and the Son and the Holy Spirit,

Matthew 28:17-19

- ***Mothering Moment***

  When a new believer confesses faith in God, am I awestruck? When my children ask God to forgive them, do I glorify God? Is glorifying God and being in awe of Him something I regularly model for my family and friends?

Praying Together
Lord, let me be filled with awe at Your presence and glory. Let me glorify Your name at every forgiven sin,

and every confession of faith, and in all discussions I hear about You.
Amen.

Week Four: Jesus Heals a Demon-Possessed Boy
(Mark 9:20-24)

Day One:
To Him (Mark 9:20)

20**They brought the boy to Him.** When he saw Him, immediately the spirit threw him into a convulsion, and falling to the ground, he began rolling around and foaming at the mouth.

21And He asked his father, "How long has this been happening to him?" And he said, "From childhood.

22"It has often thrown him both into the fire and into the water to destroy him. But if You can do anything, take pity on us and help us!"

23And Jesus said to him, " 'If You can?' All things are possible to him who believes."

24Immediately the boy's father cried out and said, "I do believe; help my unbelief."

- *Daily Truth*
  The boy had been with the disciples (except Peter, James and John) right before this part of the story unfolds. Jesus had taken the other three up on the mountain to bear witness of His Transfiguration. As Jesus was being unveiled before the three men's eyes as His heavenly self,

the other disciples were grappling with this demon-possessed boy.

After Jesus told the three not to mention the scene until after His resurrection, they all came down the mountain to return to the group. We can see that while the Lord was unveiling His majesty to a few, Satan was actively working, doing awful things at the same time. Not only that, but we can see by reading the following passages that the disciples were unable to cast out the demon, whereas they had been able to cast others out. Jesus wonders at their lack of faith, which must have been magnified in His mind, since He had just revealed His true self to Peter, James and John.

1And Jesus was saying to them, "Truly I say to you, there are some of those who are standing here who will not taste death until they see the kingdom of God after it has come with power."

2Six days later, Jesus took with Him Peter and James and John, and brought them up on a high mountain by themselves. And He was transfigured before them;

3and His garments became radiant and exceedingly white, as no launderer on earth can whiten them.

4Elijah appeared to them along with Moses; and they were talking with Jesus.

5Peter said to Jesus, "Rabbi, it is good for us to be here; let us make three tabernacles, one for You, and one for Moses, and one for Elijah."

6For he did not know what to answer; for they became terrified.

7Then a cloud formed, overshadowing them, and a voice came out of the cloud, "This is My beloved Son, listen to Him!"

8All at once they looked around and saw no one with them anymore, except Jesus alone.

9As they were coming down from the mountain, He gave them orders not to relate to anyone what they had seen, until the Son of Man rose from the dead.

Mark 9:1-9

17And one of the crowd answered Him, "Teacher, I brought You my son, possessed with a spirit which makes him mute;

18and whenever it seizes him, it slams him to the ground and he foams at the mouth, and grinds his teeth and stiffens out. I told Your disciples to cast it out, and they could not do it."

19And He answered them and said, "O unbelieving generation, how long shall I be with you? How long shall I put up with you? Bring him to Me!"

Mark 9:17-19

- ### *Mothering Moment*
   As we read in the first week about the woman with the hemorrhage, there are times when we seek other people's help before we seek the Lord's help. In this case, Jesus was not present to intervene immediately, and so His disciples were called on. We have the amazing benefit of being able to call on Jesus whenever, before we seek any kind of earthly help.   Bringing our sorrows to Him should always be our first thought, instead of falling back on Him after we have sought other help, in parenting, marriage, or any problem.

Praying Together
Lord God, I know that I need to bring all of my cares and worries to You first, before I ask for anyone's help, and before I seek advice. Father, I am sorry I don't always do that. I want You to be foremost in my mind, Jesus, so I can always remember that I need to call on You, bringing my struggles to You. I know You will always help me. Thank You, Lord.
Amen.

Week Four: Jesus Heals a Demon-Possessed Boy
(Mark 9:20-24)

Day Two:
Possessed! (Mark 9:20)

20They brought the boy to Him. **When he saw Him, immediately the spirit threw him into a convulsion, and falling to the ground, he began rolling around and foaming at the mouth.**

21And He asked his father, "How long has this been happening to him?" And he said, "From childhood.

22"It has often thrown him both into the fire and into the water to destroy him. But if You can do anything, take pity on us and help us!"

23And Jesus said to him, " 'If You can?' (A)All things are possible to him who believes."

24Immediately the boy's father cried out and said, "I do believe; help my unbelief."

- *Daily Truth*
  This boy was demon-possessed. The demon knew who Jesus was, and in reaction to seeing God's Son, threw the boy into a fit. The demon was abusing the boy in order to rebel against Jesus. Though we don't hear about a whole lot of demon possessions these days, Satan actively

uses people and situations in our lives to discourage us, distract us, and cause us to doubt who God is. Satan and his demons attack those of us who belong to Jesus as an act of rebellion and defiance. They are at war with God.

This is a vivid illustration of demon possession. There are several other examples of people being possessed by demons throughout the New Testament. These stories hold valuable truths for us because they show that we are at war once we become children of God. The demons always want to hurt and damage that which God loves.

1They came to the other side of the sea, into the country of the Gerasenes.

2When He got out of the boat, immediately a man from the tombs with an unclean spirit met Him,

3and he had his dwelling among the tombs. And no one was able to bind him anymore, even with a chain;

4because he had often been bound with shackles and chains, and the chains had been torn apart by him and the shackles broken in pieces, and no one was strong enough to subdue him.

5Constantly, night and day, he was screaming among the tombs and in the mountains, and gashing himself with stones.

6Seeing Jesus from a distance, he ran up and bowed down before Him;

7and shouting with a loud voice, he said, "What business do we have with each other, Jesus, Son of the Most High God? I implore You by God, do not torment me!"

8For He had been saying to him, "Come out of the man, you unclean spirit!"

9And He was asking him, "What is your name?" And he said to Him, "My name is Legion; for we are many."

10And he began to implore Him earnestly not to send them out of the country.

11Now there was a large herd of swine feeding nearby on the mountain.

12The demons implored Him, saying, "Send us into the swine so that we may enter them."

13Jesus gave them permission. And coming out, the unclean spirits entered the swine; and the herd rushed down the steep bank into the sea, about two thousand of them; and they were drowned in the sea.

Mark 5:1-13

13But also some of the Jewish exorcists, who went from place to place, attempted to name over those who had the evil spirits the name of the Lord Jesus, saying, "I adjure you by Jesus whom Paul preaches."

14Seven sons of one Sceva, a Jewish chief priest, were doing this.

15And the evil spirit answered and said to them, "I recognize Jesus, and I know about Paul, but who are you?"

16And the man, in whom was the evil spirit, leaped on them and subdued all of them and overpowered them, so that they fled out of that house naked and wounded.

Acts 19:13-16

- ***Mothering Moment***
  Since demons recognize Jesus, and those belonging to Him, and try to hurt and damage those belonging to Him, does that mean that they recognize me? Do they want to cause damage in my household and in my relationships? Do they want me to doubt God? Yes! We need to believe that there is a spiritual war going on around us that we cannot see. In the movie *The Usual Suspects,* Kevin Spacey's character says "the greatest trick the Devil ever pulled was convincing the world he didn't exist." If we

choose to ignore that he exists, we can never be prepared for his attacks.

Attacks will come to us. Sometimes from unexpected quarters, and through our own children and families. I find that I am most vulnerable in trying to raise my children, not in the grand scheme of things, but just in the day to day.

Praying Together
Lord God, I believe that there is a war going on around me that I cannot see. I know that You, Jesus, are the victor, and I am a part of Your conquering kingdom. I know that You will not allow Satan or his demons to ever overpower me. You are in me! Greater is He who is in me than he who is in the world. Protect me, Lord God, from the blows of the enemy. You have promised that since I belong to You, nothing will snatch me out of Your hand. I love you. Thank you for your love and protection.
Amen.

Week Four: Jesus Heals a Demon-Possessed Boy
(Mark 9:20-24)

Day Three:
Tell Me More (Mark 9:21-22)

20They brought the boy to Him. When he saw Him, immediately the spirit threw him into a convulsion, and falling to the ground, he began rolling around and foaming at the mouth.

21**And He asked his father, "How long has this been happening to him?" And he said, "From childhood.**

22**"It has often thrown him both into the fire and into the water to destroy him.** But if You can do anything, take pity on us and help us!"

23And Jesus said to him, " 'If You can?' All things are possible to him who believes."

24Immediately the boy's father cried out and said, "I do believe; help my unbelief."

- *Daily Truth*
  Jesus was demonstrating great empathy for the father of this boy. He had compassion on both of them, and He wanted to talk to the man about what had happened to his son.

There had evidently been many occasions during which this boy had endured the torture of the demon. He had been possessed for years. The demon was not going to leave the boy alone.

And His name will be called Wonderful Counselor
From Isaiah 9:6

29This also comes from the LORD of hosts,
Who has made His counsel wonderful and His wisdom great.
Isaiah 28:29

13He will have compassion on the poor and needy,
And the lives of the needy he will save.
Psalm 72:13

- ***Mothering Moment***
  I have not personally experienced the task of mothering a child with a chronic illness. Raising any child is challenging, but I have known mothers who do not go one week without a trip to the doctor or even the emergency room. The young boy in this story has a different affliction than medical childhood illnesses, but his father had certainly endured much suffering. And our Lord wanted to know more. He wanted to have the moment when the father could look into His eyes and tell Him what an ordeal it had been. Jesus wants the same moment with you. He wants to know about all our struggles, from chronic illness, to special needs, to behavior

issues.... Imagine sitting down with Jesus and explaining your child's suffering to Him. The thing is, He already knows what we go through, but we can see by this passage that He wants us to tell Him all about it.

Praying Together
Father God, I know You are already aware of everything that is happening in my life. I know that You are in control of it all. Sometimes children suffer, Lord, and we know You see it. We know You have a plan and a purpose for it. I want to pour out my heart to You when my children are hurting or suffering. You are my Wonderful Counselor. Thank You for caring so much about me and my children, and for listening when I pour out my heart to You.
Amen.

Week Four: Jesus Heals a Demon-Possessed Boy
(Mark 9:20-24)

Day Four:
If You Can? (Mark 9:22-23)

20They brought the boy to Him. When he saw Him, immediately the spirit threw him into a convulsion, and falling to the ground, he began rolling around and foaming at the mouth.

21And He asked his father, "How long has this been happening to him?" And he said, "From childhood.

22"It has often thrown him both into the fire and into the water to destroy him. **But if You can do anything, take pity on us and help us!"**

23**And Jesus said to him, " 'If You can?' All things are possible to him who believes."**

24Immediately the boy's father cried out and said, "I do believe; help my unbelief."

- *Daily Truth*
  This man still was not sure if Jesus could help his son. Have you been in those shoes? After all, Jesus' disciples couldn't help, and this man was dealing with the reality of watching his son suffer for many years. He knew that Jesus cared, and

asked for his pity. He had just enough faith, or maybe just enough desperation to think that maybe, this Jesus, who people followed and worshipped, could cast the demon out. Jesus asked the man point blank, "are you going to choose to believe me?" He was telling the man and all those looking on that skepticism and faith cannot go together. We cannot trust God, and still doubt His miraculous power, and His faith towards us.

Jesus is not saying here that anything we wish for will be granted to us if we just believe it will. This is not some strange "power of positive thinking" mantra. The "all things" Jesus speaks of here are the promises of God revealed to us through the Bible. These promises are also fulfilled in us through prayer in the Holy Spirit, and trusting that God wants what is best for His people. He will allow us to endure many things, and He will allow certain trials to come into our lives, but He has promised to deliver us and save us!

If we are faithless, He remains faithful, for He cannot deny Himself.
2 Timothy 2:13

And we know that God causes all things to work together for good to those who love God, to those who are called according to His purpose.
Romans 8:28

And He was saying, "'Abba! Father! All things are possible for You; remove this cup from Me; yet not what I will, but what You will."
Mark 14:36

- **Mothering Moment**
As a new mommy, each of the three times I was "new" I had to pray over and over again, "even when I am faithless, You remain faithful, for You cannot deny Yourself." Just the baby blues, I mean crying every time I nursed my baby, worrying that his or her life wouldn't be perfect and painless... worrying that I wasn't a good mother, that I really had no idea what I was doing... not sleeping for more than two hours at a time.... Mothering is hard, and life is hard. Mothering has helped me understand more about God, though, because I realized long ago that I couldn't be the mother I needed to be. My attitude changed from "if You can" into "You have to, because I can't, and You promised me You would."

Praying Together
Abba, Father, so many times we come to You asking "if" there is anything You can do to help us. We want You to see us, to take notice of our grief, and take pity on us. We want You to come up with some way You could possibly help! When I am tempted to ask You if You can help me, let me have faith enough to say "whatever You can do to help me, I will accept." Help me to remember that You cause all things to work together for good to

63

those who love You and are called according to Your purposes. I don't need to ask You if You can help me, but I need to be ready to accept whatever way You choose to help me.
Amen.

Week Four: Jesus Heals a Demon-Possessed Boy
(Mark 9:20-24)

Day Five:
Help My Unbelief! (Mark 9:24)

20They brought the boy to Him. When he saw Him, immediately the spirit threw him into a convulsion, and falling to the ground, he began rolling around and foaming at the mouth.

21And He asked his father, "How long has this been happening to him?" And he said, "From childhood.

22"It has often thrown him both into the fire and into the water to destroy him. But if You can do anything, take pity on us and help us!"

23And Jesus said to him, " 'If You can?' All things are possible to him who believes."

24**Immediately the boy's father cried out and said, "I do believe; help my unbelief."**

- *Daily Truth*
  The father realized immediately that he was experiencing unbelief. He confessed it and repented, asking Jesus to help his unbelief. This is an important truth in Scripture; Jesus is the source of our faith, and He is the one who

increases it in us. We cannot strive or work for faith. It comes from God alone.

22But the fruit of the Spirit is love, joy, peace, patience, kindness, goodness, faithfulness,

23gentleness, self-control; against such things there is no law.

Galatians 5:22-23

8For to one is given the word of wisdom through the Spirit, and to another the word of knowledge according to the same Spirit;

9to another faith by the same Spirit, and to another gifts of healing by the one Spirit,

10and to another the effecting of miracles, and to another prophecy, and to another the distinguishing of spirits, to another various kinds of tongues, and to another the interpretation of tongues.

I Corinthians 12:8-10

- ***Mothering Moment***

I love this verse of Scripture. It speaks to me. There is quite possibly not one day which passes that I do not cry out to Jesus saying "I do believe; help my unbelief!" Faith is a Spiritual gift. It is one of my gifts. That simply means that when the Holy Spirit came to me, He put faith into my life, as part of who I am, and as how I am supposed to serve Him in the body of believers. This is a staggering fact, because, as I said, not a day passes that it is not a struggle for me. I believe it is hard to have faith because the world causes us to question everything around us. It seems to be a highly prized attribute to be a person who has an inquisitive mind, who doesn't just take things at face value, because they will not be easily fooled. It is hard to operate as a Christian in this world, because we understand that God is in control, and not man. Putting that faith into action is difficult. Acting on our faith daily is a way of life that does not often go unchallenged by the world we live in. The good news is that faith is also a Fruit of the Spirit, evidence in our lives that Christ has redeemed us. It is possible for all believers to grow in faith, for Jesus to "help our unbelief."

Praying Together

My Lord Jesus, I do believe You. Help my unbelief! When it seems like the world around me is falling apart, help my unbelief! When my children are a trial, help my unbelief! When illness or tragedy touches someone I know, help my unbelief. I trust You, Lord, and I thank

*You for being so patient with me. Increase my faith,
please Lord, and let me stand firm on every single
promise You have made and also kept. Your faithfulness
is great towards me. Thank you, Jesus.
Amen.*

Week Five: A Mother's Request (Matthew 20:20-24)

Day One:
Bowing Down (Matthew 20:20)

20Then the mother of the sons of Zebedee came to Jesus with her sons, bowing down and making a request of Him.

21And He said to her, "What do you wish?" She said to Him, "Command that in Your kingdom these two sons of mine may sit one on Your right and one on Your left."

22But Jesus answered, "You do not know what you are asking. Are you able to drink the cup that I am about to drink?" They said to Him, "We are able."

23He said to them, "My cup you shall drink; but to sit on My right and on My left, this is not Mine to give, but it is for those for whom it has been prepared by My Father."

24And hearing this, the ten became indignant with the two brothers.

- *Daily Truth*
  Though this mother whose two sons were close followers of Jesus wanted to show Him worship and honor by bowing down to Him, her real motivation was to ask Him to do something for her. There are many times when we trade genuine worship for our own "prayer requests."

This woman was the mother of two of Jesus'
inner circle, James and John. John referred to
himself in his own gospel account as "the
disciple Jesus loved." These brothers were very
close to Jesus, and early in their ministry, they
earned the nicknames "sons of thunder." I would
assume that meant that they really were bold
about what they believed in. So, two really close
friends of Jesus who were bold and passionate
about following Him came with their mother so
she could worship Him. We know that she was
giving Him her worship by the act of bowing.
But on the heels of worshipping Him, she had a
very specific thing she wanted Him to do for her.
Her own desires overshadowed her worship of
the Lord.

*2So she ran and came to Simon Peter and to the other
disciple whom Jesus loved, and said to them, "They have
taken away the Lord out of the tomb, and we do not know
where they have laid Him."*
John 20:2

*17and James, the son of Zebedee, and John the brother of
James (to them He gave the name Boanerges, which
means, "Sons of Thunder");*
Mark 3:17

- *Mothering Moment*

I have often wondered about this situation. I mean, these are the "sons of thunder!" Surely if they had desired a special place in Jesus' kingdom they would have told Him themselves. Not to mention that they were two of Jesus' three closest friends within the twelve disciples.... I wonder because it just seems as though this mother was a little presumptive... a little pushy.... She was a mother who would do what was required to elevate her children. We have all either been there as moms, or we have seen other women do this very thing. This mom was rushing through her worship of God in order to seek a position for them in His kingdom. My hope is that we do not worship God in order for Him to do something for us, even where our children are concerned.

Praying Together
Lord God, my prayer today is this: That I would never put the needs of my children above my adoration of You. I want to come into Your presence with the willingness to submit to whatever You have for me. If that means success for my children, fine, if struggles for my children, that will have to be fine, too. I also ask that You will keep me from the temptation of pushing my children to excel, or even desiring for them to be in the limelight. I know that You will exalt the humble. Thank you for the power You give me through the Holy Spirit. Amen.

Week Five: A Mother's Request (Matthew 20:20-24)

Day Two:
What Do You Wish? (Matthew 20:21)

20Then the mother of the sons of Zebedee came to Jesus with her sons, bowing down and making a request of Him.

21**And He said to her, "What do you wish?" She said to Him, "Command that in Your kingdom these two sons of mine may sit one on Your right and one on Your left."**

22But Jesus answered, "You do not know what you are asking. Are you able to drink the cup that I am about to drink?" They said to Him, "We are able."

23He said to them, "My cup you shall drink; but to sit on My right and on My left, this is not Mine to give, but it is for those for whom it has been prepared by My Father."

24And hearing this, the ten became indignant with the two brothers.

- *Daily Truth*
  Jesus wants her to tell Him exactly what she wants. She tells Him that her sons deserve special places of honor in God's kingdom. She wants her sons to be lifted up.

Religious leaders garnered respect from people everywhere they went, and often chose for themselves seats of honor in the synagogue and at dinners. This mother was requesting the ultimate seats of honor for her sons, knowing that they were close to Jesus and respected by many who saw them and followed them. She wanted to ensure that they were well-respected.

46"Beware of the scribes, who like to walk around in long robes, and love respectful greetings in the market places, and chief seats in the synagogues and places of honor at banquets,
Luke 20:46

7And He began speaking a parable to the invited guests when He noticed how they had been picking out the places of honor at the table, saying to them,

8"When you are invited by someone to a wedding feast, do not take the place of honor, for someone more distinguished than you may have been invited by him,

9and he who invited you both will come and say to you, 'Give your place to this man,' and then in disgrace you proceed to occupy the last place.

10"But when you are invited, go and recline at the last place, so that when the one who has invited you comes, he may say to you, 'Friend, move up higher'; then you

*will have honor in the sight of all who are at the table
with you.*

*11"For everyone who exalts himself will be humbled, and
he who humbles himself will be exalted."*

Luke 14:7-11

- ### Mothering Moment
  I have one child who has made a profession of
  faith in Jesus, and two more who love to say their
  prayers and read Bible stories. Though it gives
  my heart so much joy to see them grow in faith,
  and though I desperately want them to live their
  lives glorifying God, I have to be careful not to
  think that they somehow deserve honor for loving
  Him. After all, as the puritan preacher, Thomas
  Watson said "man's chief end is to glorify God,
  and to enjoy Him forever." Children who love
  the Lord and honor Him are merely doing what
  they were created to do. As moms, we should
  encourage them, but we do not need to honor
  them, or seek honor for them.

Praying Together

*Lord God, let me live only to honor and glorify You, and
not myself. Help me to be an example to my children
that it is not Your way for us to seek honor. This world
tells us that we deserve honor and glory for doing well
and being "the best" at something. But You tell us ,
Lord Jesus, that everyone who exalts himself will be*

74

humbled, and he who humbles himself will be exalted. Help me to remember that my purpose is to glorify You and enjoy You forever, and to teach my children to do the same.

Amen.

Week Five: A Mother's Request (Matthew 20:20-24)

Day Three:
You Don't Know What You Are Asking (Matthew 20:22)

20Then the mother of the sons of Zebedee came to Jesus with her sons, bowing down and making a request of Him.

21And He said to her, "What do you wish?" She said to Him, "Command that in Your kingdom these two sons of mine may sit one on Your right and one on Your left."

22But Jesus answered, "You do not know what you are asking. Are you able to drink the cup that I am about to drink?" They said to Him, "We are able."

23He said to them, "My cup you shall drink; but to sit on My right and on My left, this is not Mine to give, but it is for those for whom it has been prepared by My Father."

24And hearing this, the ten became indignant with the two brothers.

- *Daily Truth*
  Jesus knew what belonging to the kingdom of heaven means. It requires sacrifice and selflessness, and most often persecution. He knew that He was going to give His life, and that many of His followers would do the same. The cup He refers to in this verse is martyrdom.

James and John did not understand. None of the disciples understood that Jesus was going to lay down His life, though He tried to tell them.

James and John were ready for God's kingdom to appear. They believed that Jesus was Messiah, and would usher in God's kingdom, but because they were Jewish, and were expecting a conquering king, they did not fully realize what the kingdom was going to look like. They just wanted to be conquerors like Him.

7"And as you go, preach, saying, 'The kingdom of heaven is at hand.'
Matthew 10:7

At that time the disciples came to Jesus and said, "Who then is greatest in the kingdom of heaven?"

2And He called a child to Himself and set him before them,

3and said, "Truly I say to you, unless you are converted and become like children, you will not enter the kingdom of heaven.

4"Whoever then humbles himself as this child, he is the greatest in the kingdom of heaven.

Matthew 18:1-4

- *Mothering Moment*
  The kingdom of heaven is at hand, because God is at work all the time saving people and calling them to Himself. Jesus has given us the pathway to heaven, and He allows us to participate in His work. This is the kingdom of heaven now. Being in heaven will be glorious, but instead of looking forward to receiving honor and blessing once we get there, our focus should be on giving honor and blessing once we arrive. If our focus is on ourselves, and what rewards and honors we will get, then we are still striving. It can be hard to understand this concept, let alone teach it to children, especially when we want them to do good and to do what is right in God's sight. I want my focus and my children's to be on what we can do for Jesus, always.

Praying Together

My Father, I cannot wait to be in Your presence in Heaven, not because of the streets of gold, or the mansion You have built for me, or the imperishable body, or any other perfection of life You have promised. I want to be in Your presence to daily and forever tell You just how much I love You. Help me to teach my children that though we know heaven will be magnificent, our treasure in heaven is You. Your Word tells us that as we walk in this world we will encounter persecutions. I do not know what persecutions may come, or how much worse the world will become before You rescue Your people out of it. If we are persecuted

for Your name's sake, let us count it a blessing, even if my children are persecuted.
Amen.

Week Five: A Mother's Request (Matthew 20:20-24)

Day Four:
Not Mine to Give (Matthew 20:23)

20Then the mother of the sons of Zebedee came to Jesus with her sons, bowing down and making a request of Him.

21And He said to her, "What do you wish?" She said to Him, "Command that in Your kingdom these two sons of mine may sit one on Your right and one on Your left."

22But Jesus answered, "You do not know what you are asking. Are you able to drink the cup that I am about to drink?" They said to Him, "We are able."

23He said to them, "My cup you shall drink; but to sit on My right and on My left, this is not Mine to give, but it is for those for whom it has been prepared by My Father."

24And hearing this, the ten became indignant with the two brothers.

- *Daily Truth*
  Jesus is telling the brothers that they will suffer and die for His sake, but not even He could guarantee honor for their future martyrdom. He is demonstrating His complete submission to God the Father.

The fourth chapter of Revelation paints a scene of worship around the throne of the Lamb. It describes the presence of twenty-four elders who are crowned and robed in white, who worship before the throne of the Lord always. There are twenty- four saints, out of all of human history who have the honor of sitting around the throne of God and showing Him their love and worship eternally. What a great honor. It humbles me to think that the God of the universe handpicks who will worship Him and when and how. He has selected those who will sit around the throne.

4Around the throne were twenty-four thrones; and upon the thrones I saw twenty-four elders sitting, clothed in white garments, and golden crowns on their heads. Revelation 4:4

10the twenty-four elders will fall down before Him who sits on the throne, and will worship Him who lives forever and ever, and will cast their crowns before the throne, saying,

11"Worthy are You, our Lord and our God, to receive glory and honor and power; for You created all things, and because of Your will they existed, and were created."

Revelation 4:10-11

- *Mothering Moment*
  Once we belong to God's family, He has designated a place for us in eternity. All of us. That is staggering to me. As believers, and members of the household of God, we each have a special designated role to play. He is preparing for us! That is wonderful, and causes me to praise God.

Praying Together

Almighty Father, thank You for preparing a place for me! Your great love for me is so hard for me to understand, but I believe You. I do not want to wonder about what life in heaven will be like, I just feel an overwhelming sense of honor and love that You picked me, and saved me, and You have a special role for me to play in this world and the next.. Thank You, Lord God. Amen.

Week Five: A Mother's Request (Matthew 20:20-24)

Day Five:
Indignant (Matthew 20:24)

20Then the mother of the sons of Zebedee came to Jesus with her sons, bowing down and making a request of Him.

21And He said to her, "What do you wish?" She said to Him, "Command that in Your kingdom these two sons of mine may sit one on Your right and one on Your left."

22But Jesus answered, "You do not know what you are asking. Are you able to drink the cup that I am about to drink?" They said to Him, "We are able."

23He said to them, "My cup you shall drink; but to sit on My right and on My left, this is not Mine to give, but it is for those for whom it has been prepared by My Father."

24**And hearing this, the ten became indignant with the two brothers.**

- *Daily Truth*
  The other ten disciples were not happy at all that James and John were seeking favor. The mother's request to elevate her sons caused backlash among their very closest friends.

  In previous days, we have read about how the disciples discussed who was the greatest among them. This was not the only time they felt the need for clarification. We have read that Peter, James and John were His inner circle, and they were the three that attended Him at the Transfiguration. It is highly likely, since the disciples were all human, that there was a little jealousy among the remaining ten towards these two brothers. Their mother's request only added fuel to an already existing fire.

33They came to Capernaum; and when He was in the house, He began to question them, "What were you discussing on the way?"

34But they kept silent, for on the way they had discussed with one another which of them was the greatest.

35Sitting down, He called the twelve and said to them, "If anyone wants to be first, he shall be last of all and servant of all."

Mark 9:33-35

- ***Mothering Moment***
  This mother provides a great example of what not to do to when it comes to our children's achievements. In heavenly terms, we just don't need to worry about it, because God has a role for all who love Him. But in earthly terms, we can apply this situation when our children are held up as examples or achieve some honor in life. It is so hard to do, because when my children

receive accolades, I want to boast! This passage teaches us that encouraging our children to seek honor will only hurt their relationships. James' and John's mother really could have done damage to the earthly ministry Jesus had to accomplish. One mother's meddling could have caused a rift between the chosen preachers of the Gospel. Let us learn from her mistake and teach our children not to seek honor, and let us not seek honor for them.

Praying Together

Lord, I know that I become indignant with some people when they achieve great things. I envy other women for their accomplishments, and sometimes I envy other people for how their children act or behave, or achieve. Envy causes discontent, and it is not Your will for me to be discontented with all of the bountiful blessings You pour out on me. Please teach me to not become jealous or indignant with others, and not to foster strife within any group of people, especially if they are ministering to others. I am sorry for my sins of envy and jealousy. Thank You for forgiving me, Lord God.
Amen.

Week Six: The Easy Yoke (Matthew 11:28-30)

Day One:
Come to Me (Matthew 11:28)

28"**Come to Me, all who are weary and heavy-laden,** and I will give you rest.

29"Take My yoke upon you and learn from Me, for I am gentle and humble in heart, and YOU WILL FIND REST FOR YOUR SOULS.

30"For My yoke is easy and My burden is light."

- ***Daily Truth***
  Jesus is giving us a command. He wants us to come to Him in order to learn His ways. But notice who He is addressing: Those who are weary and heavy-laden. The truth of this statement is that not all will follow Him because not all people realize that they are heavy-laden.

  Jesus spoke these words in the hearing of many people, mostly Jews. He praised God for revealing the Gospel to people who did not have great learning, but were infants in faith. Many of the people hearing Him would not have considered themselves in need of any kind of spiritual help.

25At that time Jesus said, "I praise You, Father, Lord of heaven and earth, that You have hidden these things from the wise and intelligent and have revealed them to infants.

26"Yes, Father, for this way was well-pleasing in Your sight.

27"All things have been handed over to Me by My Father; and no one knows the Son except the Father; nor does anyone know the Father except the Son, and anyone to whom the Son wills to reveal Him.

Matthew 11:25-27

- ***Mothering Moment***
  I believe that Jesus spoke these words knowing that women would hear Him, and I sense that He is speaking directly to us, even now, in this generation of women. Out of all people and all occupations, women, mothers in particular, are the most weary and heavy-laden. We are tired from taking care of our families, and from meeting everyone's high expectations, and heavy-laden by the responsibility for little peoples' lives. He meant these words for us! We are special to Him, and He wants us to come to Him!

Praying Together
Thank You, Lord Jesus, for knowing that I am weary and heavy-laden, and thank You for calling me to come to You. I accept Your invitation. I am following You, because I am weary and heavy-laden.
Amen.

Week Six: The Easy Yoke (Matthew 11:28-30)

Day Two:
Rest (Matthew 11:28)

28"Come to Me, all who are weary and heavy-laden, **and I will give you rest.**

29"Take My yoke upon you and learn from Me, for I am gentle and humble in heart, and YOU WILL FIND REST FOR YOUR SOULS.

30"For My yoke is easy and My burden is light."

- *Daily Truth*
  This is another great promise of Scripture, and a great example of God's faithfulness. Jesus has promised to give us rest. He does not intend that we should never work, or work hard. Rest in this sense means that we can live and work and minister without the added weight of worry and anxiety. The literal translation from the Greek is the word "refreshed."

  Just like in our current age, people during Jesus' time on earth were striving. People did not, and still do not regularly look for rest. Especially in the ancient Jewish worship of God, most of the focus was on the acts and the offerings the people did for God, not resting in His presence. People get tired, especially moms, but it is fundamentally true that mankind strives for things, whether work, money, pleasure, and even religion. Rest simply does not come naturally to us.

10*"Cease striving and know that I am God;*
    I will be exalted among the nations, I will be
exalted in the earth."
Psalm 46:10

- ### *Mothering Moment*
    How many of us would love to go about our days as mothers "refreshed." Could we be better mothers and better wives if we accepted the rest Jesus offers to us daily? How can I cease striving, come to Jesus and be refreshed today?

Praying Together
Jesus, I do want the refreshment You are offering. I know that You will empower me through the Holy Spirit to work and minister and nurture and teach without worrying and being anxious about my work. Please fill me up today with Your presence, Lord God. I accept the gift of rest and refreshment You are giving me. I give up on striving and worrying. I will rely on You.
Amen.

Week Six: The Easy Yoke (Matthew 11:28-30)

Day Three:
The Easy Yoke (Matthew 11:29)

28"Come to Me, all who are weary and heavy-laden, and I will give you rest.

29**"Take My yoke upon you and learn from Me,** for I am gentle and humble in heart, and YOU WILL FIND REST FOR YOUR SOULS.

30"For My yoke is easy and My burden is light."

- *Daily Truth*
  Jesus is asking us to take a yoke on; this is an expression of work. Being a follower of Christ is not all rest and refreshment . He is telling us to take on His work, the work of the kingdom of heaven. Loving God, and loving one another, and sharing the Truth of God's Word with the world. That was Jesus' work, and it needs to be ours as well. He doesn't ask us to do it alone, He tells us we will learn how to do it by spending time with Him.

  Jesus was using a common agricultural illustration here. His audience would have been familiar with the use of yokes in putting oxen to work. If you've seen a few episodes of *Little House on the Prairie,* this will be familiar to you. Oxen worked in teams, one older and more experienced, and one younger, needing to be trained. They were placed in the same yoke, a type of harness, with the more experienced ox on the steering side. He did the leading, and the younger ox learned from Him. Jesus wants to lead us, and train us, by walking with us daily and teaching us how to do the work set before us.

26In the same way the Spirit also helps our weakness; for we do not know how to pray as we should, but the Spirit Himself intercedes for us with groanings too deep for words;

27and He who searches the hearts knows what the mind of the Spirit is, because He intercedes for the saints according to the will of God.

Romans 8:26-27

- ***Mothering Moment***
  Is it a refreshing idea to think of Jesus walking by your side every day, leading you and teaching you how to be the mother your child needs you to be? Do you believe that He can and will teach you how to be a mother and a wife?

  Sometimes we think of Jesus as being far off, away from us, still accessible somehow, but nevertheless removed from our current circumstances. I heard a great teacher,

Priscilla Shirer, at a MOPS convention
several years ago say that when we pray, we
should envision Jesus sitting right next to us,
praying for us and along with us. I still try to
do that at least once a day, and my soul is
refreshed.

Praying Together

*Lord Jesus, I know that even now, it is as though You are
sitting here in this room with me. You will walk with me
and lead me and teach me. You painted a picture of two
oxen working together as a team to accomplish their
work, the stronger leading the weaker. Thank You ,
Lord, for being stronger than I ever can be. Thank You,
for being willing to lead me and teach me. I want to take
on Your yoke today, and do Your work.*
Amen.

Week Six: The Easy Yoke (Matthew 11:28-30)

Day Four:
Humble in Heart (Matthew 11:29)

28"Come to Me, all who are weary and heavy-laden, and I will give you rest.

29"Take My yoke upon you and learn from Me, **for I am gentle and humble in heart, and YOU WILL FIND REST FOR YOUR SOULS.**

30"For My yoke is easy and My burden is light."

- *Daily Truth*
  Jesus tells us the key to being the mothers and wives God calls us to be: we must learn from Him how to be gentle and humble in heart. We have to receive it from Him, because there is no other way to be truly gentle, or humble.

  Being gentle and humble in heart is another way of stating the greatest commandments; (to love God, and to love our neighbors as ourselves.) In gentleness, we can love people, and in a humble heart, we can really love God and pay tribute to who He is. Once again, Jesus tells us that this will bring rest to our souls, referencing the prophet Jeremiah.

36"Teacher, which is the great commandment in the Law?"

37And He said to him, " 'YOU SHALL LOVE THE LORD YOUR GOD WITH ALL YOUR HEART, AND WITH ALL YOUR SOUL, AND WITH ALL YOUR MIND.'

38"This is the great and foremost commandment.

39"The second is like it, 'YOU SHALL LOVE YOUR NEIGHBOR AS YOURSELF.'

40"On these two commandments depend the whole Law and the Prophets."
Matthew 22:36-40

3Your adornment must not be merely external--braiding the hair, and wearing gold jewelry, or putting on dresses;

4but let it be the hidden person of the heart, with the imperishable quality of a gentle and quiet spirit, which is precious in the sight of God.
I Peter 3:3-4

16Thus says the LORD,
"Stand by the ways and see and ask for the ancient paths,
Where the good way is, and walk in it;

And you will find rest for your souls.

But they said, 'We will not walk in it.'
Jeremiah 6:16

- ### *Mothering Moment*
  Being a mother forces us to walk a tightrope
  between humbling ourselves daily to put the
  needs of others ahead of our own, (cleaning
  up any sort of bodily fluid is pretty
  humbling,) and comparing ourselves to
  everyone around us, to see how they're
  getting along. This is not true humility. It is
  also a challenge to be gentle with our children
  in the day to day struggle, particularly in the
  area of discipline. Being gentle as we rock
  our babies to sleep is one thing, but after the
  third consecutive time-out (or spanking,)
  there are few who can remain gentle. Jesus
  is not suggesting that we copy Him, though.
  Just as we saw a couple of days ago, He
  wants us to cease striving. When we try to be
  gentle and humble, it is our own strength, not
  His. It is only through being born again that
  our hearts, made new by God, can be gentle
  and humble.

Praying Together
Lord, today it is my prayer that if there is a woman
reading this book who has never accepted Your gift of
salvation, through the sacrifice and resurrection of
Jesus, Your Son, that she would do it today. The only
way to be gentle and humble in heart is to get a new

heart from You, Lord God. Please let that happen in someone's life today.
Amen.

Week Six: The Easy Yoke (Matthew 11:28-30)

Day Five:
How Can a Burden be Light? (Matthew 11:30)

28"Come to Me, all who are weary and heavy-laden, and I will give you rest.

29"Take My yoke upon you and learn from Me, for I am gentle and humble in heart, and YOU WILL FIND REST FOR YOUR SOULS.

30"**For My yoke is easy and My burden is light.**"

- *Daily Truth*
  Jesus is referring to His work (His yoke.) It is still work, to do the things of God, but it is His work, and so we do it in His strength. *Webster's Dictionary* defines burden: "something that is carried," and "something oppressive or worrisome." How can a burden be light? When we fully submit to carrying out God's will for our lives, and when we choose each day to seek Jesus and stand in the knowledge that He can do all things. Jesus is not saying that our burdens will be light, but that His is. The point is to refocus our striving from our own work to the work of the Lord, then He will bear it with us, and it will be light.

A burden instantly becomes lighter when it is shared. Jesus always did the will of the Father, which made His work easy for Him, because He knew that God would never leave Him. The work Jesus did was to restore God's people to Himself. He could call it "easy" and "light" because He was carrying out God's will.

13I can do all things through Him who strengthens me.
Philippians 4:13

"For the Son of Man has come to seek and to save that which was lost."
Luke 19:10

- ***Mothering Moment***
  When we take on the burden of being a mom, we know that Jesus is shouldering the burden with us, which makes it instantly lighter. But there is a greater burden Jesus speaks of, and that is seeking out lost people and telling them about God. As moms, we have at least one person in our lives who needs to hear about God's salvation; our child. Because we are moms, we come into contact with all sorts of people who are going to need to hear about God's salvation. This is the easy yoke and the light burden. A Sunday School teacher once told a classroom full of young married couples that once you start doing God's work,

and prioritizing your life around Him,
everything else falls into place, and many
things fall away. Have you tried on the easy
yoke?

Praying Together
*Lord God, I understand that You have put me on this
earth to save me, so that I can glorify You and do Your
will. Your work is to tell others about You. You came to
seek and save that which is lost. Let me take up Your
burden, and feel how light it is. This is my purpose.
Thank You for saving me, Jesus.*
Amen.